LETTERS ON THE
COUNCIL OF EPHESUS

Capreolus,
Bishop of Carthage

Translated by: D.P. Curtin

Dalcassian Publishing Company
PHILADELPHIA, PA

LETTERS ON THE COUNCIL OF EPHESUS

Copyright @ 2007 Dalcassian Publishing Company

All rights reserved. No part of this publication may be reproduced, distributed, or transmitted in any form or by any means, including photocopying, recording, or other electronic or mechanical methods, without the prior written permission of the publisher, except in the case of brief quotations embodied in critical reviews and certain other non-commercial uses permitted by copyright law. For permission request, write to Dalcassian Publishing Company at dalcassianpublishing at gmail.com

ISBN: 979-8-8691-5846-8 (Paperback)

Library of Congress Control Number:
Author: Curtin, D.P. (1985-)

Printed by Ingram Content Group, 1 Ingram Blvd, La Vergne, Tennessee

First printing edition 2007.

LETTERS ON THE COUNCIL OF EPHESUS

THE FIRST LETTER TO THE COUNCIL OF EPHESUS
Concerning the one person of Christ, God and man, against Nestorius.

I. I wished, most pious brethren, that your venerable synod had been assembled in such a state of affairs, that it would have allowed us also, having chosen by common opinion some of our brothers and co-bishops, to send an informed delegation rather than an apology worthy of lamentation, unless this affection of our mind had been hindered by a different cause. For the first of the letters delivered to our hands by our most pious lord and son Theodosius, the emperor, were of such a kind as to lament the presence of the blessed memory of our brother and co-bishop Augustine in a special way. However, when those letters had discovered that he had already passed away from life, I, receiving that royal meaning, although it seemed particularly intended for the aforesaid Augustine, sent to all the provinces of Africa appropriate letters and customary speeches, I wanted to compel a suitable synod; by which, of course, some would be selected from the number of our brothers and bishops, who would be destined for your venerable beatitude's synod. But all access to the road was blocked by this storm. Indeed, the scattered multitude of the enemy, and the immense desolation of the provinces everywhere, which, with the inhabitants partly exterminated and partly put to flight, presents to the eye a miserable appearance of desolation, stretching far and wide in every direction, and restrains that ready opportunity of coming. By these impediments, therefore, the bishops whose object was to be forbidden, were unable to assemble together from the region of Africa. In addition to these difficulties, the emperor's letter was brought to us in the days of Easter, when there were scarcely two months left until the venerable universal synod. The interval of time, of course, even if there had been no difficulty in the absence of the enemy, was hardly sufficient to compel the African synod. Hence it came about that, although we did not intend to send any solemn message, nevertheless, out of reverence and respect due to ecclesiastical discipline, we sent my son Besula, the deacon, together with these letters of apology to you, venerable brothers.

II. Wherefore I desire to beseech your Holiness again and again (even though the Catholic faith, through so great a synod of venerable priests, I trust with the help of our God to be stable and firm in all things,) that with the cooperation of the Holy Spirit, who, I have no doubt, will be available to your hearts in all that you are about to do, new doctrines, and heretofore unknown to ecclesiastical ears, having been armed from the midst with the strength of ancient authority, and thus resisting any new errors; lest the authority of the apostolic see, and the unanimous opinion of the priests, oppress those whom the Church had long attacked, and in these times repulsed, should seem to renew the voice which had long since been taken away under the pretext of a second discussion. For if by any chance new controversies arise, it must be submitted to discussion, so that either what has been rightly said may be proved, or it may be exploded as worthy of condemnation. But indeed, if anyone allows things which have already been decided once more to be called into discussion; Of course, he will be considered to be doing nothing else than to doubt himself about the faith that has prevailed up to now. Then, as an example to posterity, that those things which are now defined as the Catholic faith, may be able to obtain perpetual firmness; it is necessary to preserve unshaken and immovable all those things which were established by the holy Fathers in former times. For he who wishes to retain that perpetual stability which he has established on the basis of the Catholic faith, must corroborate his opinion, not by his own authority, but by the judgment of the ancient Fathers: so that, confirming his pleas partly by ancient, partly by more recent decrees and opinions, the one truth of the Church has since from the beginning to the present time, proceeding with simple purity and invincible constancy and authority, let him show himself to assert, to teach, and to hold. I wished to suggest this to your venerable ears for the present delegation of Africans, which was prevented by the necessity mentioned above. In the meantime, I implore you that, considering the calamities of things and the present times, you would ascribe our absence not to pride or negligence, but to this manifest necessity. Cyril, bishop of the Church of Alexandria, said: And this letter of the most reverend and most pious bishop of Carthage, Capreolus, which was read, since it contains a clear sentence in itself, is inserted in the acts of faith. For he wants the old dogmas of the faith to be confirmed, and the new ones, which have been thought up absurdly and spread impiously, to be rejected and proscribed.

All the bishops cried out together. These are the voices of all: these we all affirm. This is the wish of all:

Ηὐχόμην, εὐλαβέστατοι ἀδελφοὶ, ἐν τοιαύτῃ καταστάσει τὴν προσκυνητὴν ὑμῶν σύνοδον συγκροτηθῆναι, ἵνα καὶ ἡμεῖς ἐπιλεχθέντων κοινῇ κρίσε ι ἀδελφῶν καὶ συνεπισκόπων ἡμετέρων, οὐ παραίτησιν θρήνου ἀξίαν, ἀλλὰ παρεσκευασμένην μᾶλλον πρεσβείαν πέμψωμεν · εἰ μὴ τὴν ἡμετέραν σύσ τασιν αἰτίαι διάφοροι ἐνεπόδιζον. Καὶ γὰρ πρῶτον τοῦ δεσπότου καὶ υἱοῦ ἡμετέρου τοῦ εὐσεβεστάτου βασιλέως Θεοδοσίου Τοιαῦτα εἰς τὰς ἡμετέρας χεῖρας γράμματα ἐλήλυθεν, ἅ τινα τοῦ τῆς μακαρίας μνήμης ἀδελφοῦ ἡμετέρου καὶ συνεπισκόπου αὐγουστίνου τὴν παρουσίαν ἰδικῶς ἀπῄτει · ἅ τινα προειρημένα γράμματα εἰς ταύτην τὴν ζῶην εὑρεῖν αὐτὸν οὐδαμῶς δεδύνηντα. Ὅθεν ἐγὼ, ὅς τις τὴν αὐτὴν βασιλίωσιν, εἰ καὶ τὰ ἄλιστα τῷ προειρημένῳ πεπεμφθαι ἐδόκει, ἐδεξάμην καταπεμφθεῖσαν, κατὰ πάσας τὰς ἐπαρχίας τῆς Ἀφρικῆς τοῖς ἁρμοδίοις γράμμασι, καὶ ταῖς ἐθίμοις χεράσεσι συναδουσαν ἡβουλήθην συναγαγεῖν, ριθμοῦ τῶν ἀδελφῶν καὶ ἐπισκοπων τῶν ἡμετερόν εἰς τὴν προσκυνητὴν σύνοδον τῆς ὑμετερας μακαριότητος καταπεμφθῶσιν. Ἀλλ᾽ ἐπειδὴ οὐκ ἀνέῳκται ἡ εἴσοδος τῆς παροδίας · καὶ γὰρ ἡ ἐπιχυθεῖσα πολεμία πληθὺς, καὶ ἡ πόρθησις ἡ πλατεῖα τῶν ἐπαρχιῶν, ἤ τις ἢ ἀποσβ εσθέντων τῶν οἰκητόρων, ἢ φυγόντων, ἀθλίαν ἐρημώσεως ὄψιν εἰς μῆκος καὶ πλάτος ἐκτείνουσα, τὴν εὐχέρειαν συστέλλει τοῦ ἐλθεῖν. Τούτοις τοιγαροῦν τοῖς κωλύμασι συνελθεῖν εἰς ἓν τοῦ κικρό τῆς Ἀφρικῆς οἱ ἐπίσκοποι οὐδαμῶς ἠδυνήθησαν, οἷς προετέθη. Ἐπειδὴ τὰ βασιλικὰ γράμματα ἐν ἡμέραις τοῦ πάσχα εἰς ἡμᾶς ἦλθε, ὅτε μόλις μέχρι τῆς πρόσκυνητῆς πάσης συνόδου δύο μηνῶν διάστημα περιελι μπάνετο οἵ τινες μόλις ἤρκουν, κἂν αὐτῇ τῇ κατὰ ἀφρικὴν συνόδῳ εἰς τὸ συνελθεῖν, καὶ εἰ μηδεμία δυσχέρεια ἀπὸ τῶν πολεμίων ἡ παροῦσα συμβεβήκει ἐντεῦθεν γεγενῆσθαι · Ἵνα, εἰ καὶ τὰ μάλιστα πρέσβεις οὐδαμῶς ἐκπέμψαι δεδυνήμεθα, διὰ τὴν εὐλάβειαν ὅμως τὴν χπεωστουμένην τῇ ἐκκλησιαστικῇ ἐπιστήμῃ, τὸν υ ἱὸν τὸν ἐμὸν βεσούλαν τὸν διάκονον μετὰ τούτων τῶν τῆς παραιτήσεως γραμμάτων ἐπέμψαμεν, προσκυνητοὶ ἀδελφοί.

Ὅθαεν αἰτῶ τὴν ὑμετέραν ἁγιότητα · εἰ καὶ τὰ μάλιστα πιστεύω τῇ βοηθείᾳ τοῦ ἡμετέρου θεοῦ, τοσαύτην σύνοδον προσκυνητῶν ἱερέων βεβαίαν διὰ π άντων τὴν πίστιν τὴν καθολικὴν ἐσομένην · ἵνα, ἐνεργοῦντος τοῦ ἁγίου πνεύματος, ὅπερ ταῖς ὑμετέραις καρδίαις ἐν πᾶσι τοῖς πρακτέοις πιστεύομ εν παρεσόμενον, τὰς καινὰς διδασκαλίας, καὶ πρὸ τούτου ταῖς ἐκκλησιαστικαῖς ἀκοαῖς ἀπείρους, τῆς ἀρχαίας αὐθεντίας τῇ δυνάμει ἀπώσησθε, καὶ οὕτω ταῖς καιναῖς οἰαισδήπ Οτε πλάναις ἀντιστῆτε · ἵνα μὴ τούτους, οὓς πάλαι ἐπολέμησεν ἡ ἐκκλησία, καὶ τούτοις τοῖς καιροῖς ἐν οἷς ἀνεφύησαν, καὶ τῆς ἀποστολικῆς ἀποστολικῆς ἀποστολικῆς καθέ καθέ δρας ἡ αὐθεντὶα; καὶ εἰς ἓν συμφονοῦσα ἡ ψῆφος ἡ ἱερατικὴ συνέχωσεν, ἐν προσχήματι δευτερας χεράσεως ἡ φωνὴ δόξη, ἡ πάλαι ἀναιρεθεῖσα, ἀνανεοῦσθαι. Ἔχει γὰρ, εἴ τι τυχὸν νεωστὶ ἀναφυῇ, ζητήσεως ἀνάγκην, ἵνα ἢ λεχθέν γομασθῇ, ἢ καταδικασθὲν δυνηθῇ ἀποκρήσθῆναι. Ταῦτα δὲ περὶ ὧν ἤδη πάλαι ἐκρίθη ἐάν τις ἐπαφῇ εἰς δευτέραν διάλεξιν κληθῆναι, οὐδὲν ἕτερον δόξει, ἢ περὶ τῆς πίστεως, ἥ τις πάκης δεῦρο κατέσχεν, αὐτὸς ἀμφιβάλλειν. Ἔπειτα διὰ τὸ τῶν μεταγενεστέρων ὑπό· ἵνα ταῦτα ἅπερ νῦν ὑπὲρ τῆς καθολικῆς πίστεως ὥρισται, ἔχειν δυνηθῇ διηνεκῆ βεβαίωσιν, ταῦτα ἥπερ ἤδη ἐστὶ παρὰ τῶν πατέρων ὁρισθέντα, φυλακτέα ἐστίν. Ἐπειδὴ ὅστις βούλεται, ἱερ ὑρὲρ τῆς καθολικῆς καταστάσεως ἐθέσπισεν, εἰς τὸ διηνεκὲς μένειν, οὐ τῇ ἰδίᾳ αὐθεντιᾳ, ἀλλὰ καὶ τῇ τῶν ἰρχαιοτέρων ψηφῳ ὀφείλει τεβαρωθῆναι ὅπερ εφρονησεν· ὥστε τούτος τοῦτο μὲν ἀπὸ τῶν ἐρχαιτέρων, διαβεβαιοῦται, δοκιμάζων, μονογενῆ τῆς καθολικῆς ἐκκλησίας τὴν ἀλήθειαν, ἀπὸ τῶν παρῳχημένων καιρῶν πάκηση τῶν παρόντων ἤτοι τῶν ἡμετέρων, ἁπλῇ καθαρτητι, καὶ ἀηττήτῳ αὐθεντίᾳ καὶ τῆς καὶ. ἑαυτὸν καὶ λέγειν, καὶ διδάξειν, καὶ κατάκειν. Ταῦτα τέως ὑπὲρ τῆς παρούσης πρεσβείας τῆς Ἀφρικῆς, ἥν τινα καταπέμψαι ἡ ἀνάγκη ἡ προρρηθεῖσα οὐ σεχώρησε, ταῖς προσκυνηταῖς ὑμῶν ἀκοαῖς ὑπέβαλον, πλεῖστα παρακαλῶν, ἵνα τεωρηθεισῶν τῶν ἐν τοῖς πάγωσι καὶ καιροῖς συμφορῶν, ἢ ἀμελείᾳ ἀλλὰ ταύτῃ τῇ προδήλῳ ἀνάγκῃ μᾶλλον λογίσασθαι καταξιώσητε.

Κύριλλος ἐπίσκοπος Ἀλεξανδρείας εἶπε· Καὶ ἡ ἀναγνωσθεῖσα ἐπιστολὴ τοῦ εὐλαβεστάτου καὶ θεοφιλεστάτου ἐπισκοπου τῆς Καρθαγένης Καπραιολου ἐμφερέσθω τῇ πίστει τῶν ὑπομνημάτων, φανερὰν ἔχουσα διάνοιαν. Βούλεται γὰρ, τὰ μὲν ἀρχαῖα κρατύνεσθαι τῆς πίστεως δόγματα, τὰ δὲ γανά, καὶ ἀτόπος ἐξευρημένα. καὶ ἀσεβῶς εἰρημένα, ἀποδοκιμάζεσθαι καὶ ἐκβάλλεσθαι.

Πάντες οἱ ἐπίσκοποι ἀνεφώνησαν· αὗται πάντων αἱ φωναί· ταῦτα πάντες λέγομεν· αὕτη πάντων ἡ εὐχή.

EPISTLE II: LETTER OF THE SERVANTS OF GOD, VITALIS AND CONSTANTIUS OF SPAIN, TO CAPREOLUS, BISHOP OF THE CATHOLIC CHURCH OF CARTHAGE.

To the Lord and to the most venerable and most blessed servant of God in Christ, our lord and God, Vitalis and Constantius sinners.

I. These are the first wishes of our humility. Sir Father This indeed was much of our desire, to write to your holy honor through our sweetest brother Numinianus. For our smallness has found the excellent reputation and teaching of your holiness: through which we write of your blessedness, as the Psalmist says: Their voice went out into all the earth, and their words to the ends of the earth (Ps. 18:5). We also ask your honor to command that our bowels be irrigated from the good treasure of your heart, which the Catholic faith holds true. Because there are some here who say that God should not be called born. For this is also their belief, that a pure man was born of the virgin Mary, and that after this God dwelt in him. To whose affirmation we, your humble children, resist, it should not be said so: but we confess, as the evangelist says, when the angel Gabriel announced to Mary, saying: The Holy Spirit will come upon you, and the power of the Most High will overshadow you.

II. Let us therefore confess that God was in the womb of the virgin Mary, that He assumed some part, that He fashioned God for Himself a man, that He was born a true God and a true man whom He assumed for the salvation of the human race, as the Apostle says: When the fullness of the time had come, God sent forth His Son, made of a woman, made under the law, that he might redeem those who were under the law (Gal. 4:4). And again: But feel this in yourselves, as also in Christ Jesus: who, being in the form of God, did not presumptuously presume to be equal to God: but emptied himself, taking the form of a servant, being made in the likeness of men, and found in the habit of a man. He humbled himself by becoming obedient unto death, and the death of the cross (Phil. 2:5-8). And again: the Mediator of God and men, the man Christ Jesus (1 Tim. 2:5). Because the mediator can no longer be called God purely without the man whom he assumed, nor man without God: because the signification of the mediator is twofold in one person, God and man: whereas God is God from God, and according to the flesh he is the same son of man. Therefore, this mediator is true God and true man, just as the form of God and the form of man. For even at the beginning of the beginning to the Romans, the holy apostle says thus: What he had promised before through his prophets in the holy Scriptures concerning his Son, who was made to him of the seed of David according to the flesh: who was predestined to be the Son of God in power according to the spirit of sanctification, from the resurrection of the dead. Jesus Christ our Lord (Rom. 1, 2-4). It is also true that Isaiah, the author of the prophets, says thus: Behold, a virgin shall conceive in her womb, and bear a son, and you shall call his name Emmanuel, which is translated, God with us (Isaiah 7:14; Matt. 1:23). But they also say that the pure man hung on the cross: they say, God departed from him. To whom our littleness says thus, God never withdrew from a man taken up, except when he said from the cross: *Heli, Heli, Lamma Sabactani*: God, my God, why have you forsaken me (Matt. 27:46)? And therefore, bowing down on our knees, let us, your humble servants, implore your holy apostleship, that you may inform us of our smallness in these things which the Catholic faith holds right; The Lord Christ is able to grant us forgiveness through your holy prayers, so that we do not descend into the depths of evil. Pray for us, holy lord, venerable and most blessed pope.

May our Lord Jesus keep your venerability safe for us longer, holy lord and venerable pope.

EPISTLE II, OR A REPRESENTATION TO VITAL AND CONSTANT.
On the one true person of Christ, God and man, against the recently condemned heresy of Nestorius.

To the most beloved and religious sons of Vitalis and Constantius, Capreolus, bishop.

I. Having received and read your letters, which you sent through the religious man Numinian, my dearest son, to your safety and diligence, in which you hold and defend with inviolable piety the established and ancient rule of the Catholic faith, I am greatly congratulated, I warn you of the Nestorian heresy, a new and strange perdition, as in some places it had already begun to sprout, with you also wanting to lay the seeds of its weed in the hearts of experts. I truly believe and trust that our Lord, the creator of all, has a perfect farmer in every place of his dominion, and that he has always had workers worthy of the evangelical harvest; who, although the impure seeds should not be rooted out before the time of fall, yet they are always on the watch with continuous prayers and preaching: so that even these, if it could be done while there is time, may be converted and changed into wheat; to stifle the adulterous intermingling. For already, as I have no doubt that it has also reached your notice, within the parts of the East, where this pestilence first arose, a glorious synod of priests was assembled, to which also our delegation was not absent, pressed in the entrance with its author and asserter, and the ray of the apostolic light was extinguished. Nor should your charity be surprised, if, even after its damnation, among the dying spirits, the stinking spirit still draws its breath. For the audacity of heretics is always obstinate, and they persist in their evil destruction by the pressing weight of sins. If perhaps you have not yet known, you will be able to recognize it with an easy reading.

II. Therefore, although the universal authority of the Church itself is fully sufficient for Christian and devout minds, nor yours, in so far as the message sent by you has been permitted, in this case the assertion seems less: nevertheless, let me not also think it necessary to deny the answer to the holy petition and question, and that this is one true doctrine let us confess how much evangelical antiquity holds and delivers. That is: that the Son of God, the true God, and the true man, is one completely and inseparable person: neither as in other patriarchs, prophets, apostles, and other holy and most illustrious men did God dwell or dwells, so In Christ Jesus we believe that divine fullness came as it were from without; but in a proper and ineffable way, the Son of God also became the son of man: so that he who was begotten by the substance of the Father continued and continues to be the only begotten, being wonderfully received by man, became the firstborn among many brothers (Rom. 8:29): and who was in the beginning the Word, and the Word was with God, and God was the Word, the Word would become flesh and dwell in us (John 1:1, 14). From which, therefore, the mystery which was hidden from the ages (Col. 1, 26) in God, began through an angel in the womb to work for a virgin, and the Holy Spirit came upon her, and the power of the Most High overshadowed her (Luke 1:35); God condescended to be born in man, who always was, that man might be born, such as he had not been before. or we do not in any way believe that a person can be divided between God and man: lest in the divinity a Trinity should be reckoned, but a quaternity. heavenly: such as is earthly, such also are earthly; and such as are heavenly, such also are heavenly: as we have borne the image of the earthly, let us also bear the image of him who is from heaven (1 Cor. 15:47-49). or what distinction is there between flesh and blood in the man Adam, and in the man Christ, if this man is not full of God? For what does the second man from heaven mean to himself? But because the Word was made flesh (John 1:14), therefore he was called a heavenly man. Nor therefore did he have true flesh, because he came down from heaven, because God took flesh. The Lord said the same about himself: No one ascends into heaven, but he who descends from heaven, the Son of Man who is in heaven (John 3:13). and had ascended to the glory of the resurrection: and yet he said that the son of man was already in heaven. This, of course, testifying to all truth, because both for man's sake God dwelt on earth, and for God's sake man dwelt in heaven. Hence also the apostle says: He who descends is himself and who ascended above all the heavens, that he might fulfill all things (Ephesians 4:10). Also elsewhere, when the Savior himself spoke mystically about the food of his flesh and the drink of his blood, knowing that his disciples were offended by this and murmured, saying: This is a hard work, who can listen to him (John 6:61)? Thus, he says: This offends you? If you then see the son of man ascending where he was before (Ibid., 63)? Behold, you also notice here how because of the unity of God and the person of man, the son of man goes where he was before to ascend, which is evidently formed in the womb of a virgin, so that from it he took the beginning of human birth. in the same way, God cannot be separated from what has happened to man or around man. Therefore, man was born who had not yet been, because the Word became flesh and dwelt among us (John 1:14). the suffering man whom he took up, and died immortal, and rose again who never dies. For God was not lacking in that man even in passion: otherwise, the Lord of glory would not have been crucified (1 Cor. 2:8). or indeed is it to be feared, lest the divinity be there as if in punishment, whom no quality affects, no madness limits? Resolve, as it is written, the births of the underworld, in which the Lord of things willed and as he willed, he could not subject himself to such a condition (Acts 2:24). He would proclaim, accumulating this also among his innumerable powers: Have you taken away the light from the wicked, or broken the arm of the proud? Or have you come to the ends of the sea? Or have you walked in the footsteps of the abyss? Or have you known the breadth under heaven (Job 38:15-18)? If this is the voice of the Father, then nothing is difficult for the Almighty, since he is everywhere, he is nowhere. with thy spirit, and from thy face whither shall I flee? If I ascend into heaven, thou art there; if I descend into hell, thou art gone (Ps. 38: 7, 8). Witnessing and demonstrating this completely, God, whose majesty is full of all things, participates in a certain incomprehensible and inexplicable way even in hell. concerning him so much was foretold in prophecy, and the voice of the Son of God was fulfilled, because by him all things were made, and without him nothing was made (John 1:3): he himself is in man deigned to visit the underworld, obstructed, and those in charge by the presence of death He was terrified by the invincible majesty, and for the sake of liberating those whom he wished, he ordered the gates of the underworld to be opened.

V. Indeed, John the Apostle speaks of him in the Apocalypse thus: He laid his right hand on me, saying: Fear not: I am the first and the last; and the living, who had been dead; and behold, I am alive forever and ever: and I have the key of death and hell (Apoc. 1, 17, 18). He was not deigned to take up the cross and death for us. And therefore, to whom in the Divinity all creatures are naked, even in man he has taken up the keys of death and hell. so that we do not believe the very soul of the assumption, either perishably received, or tenaciously abandoned. But neither do we believe his flesh infected with the contagion of any corruption. Psal.15, 10; Act.2, 28). He himself became like a man without a helper because of our guilt (Ps. 87: 6): but because of his innocence and power he was found free among the dead. As it is written (Ps. 68:5) he was dissolving. It is not surprising, therefore, if a place receives God, and yet does not grasp it: it feels the presence, does not hinder the majesty: it frightens the omnipotence, does not include the substance. perhaps the light], nor be obscured by darkness, nor varied in places, nor affected by passions, nor diminished by conditions, nor changed by times. resurrected (Matt. 27:51, 52), if God visited the underworld at all? Who is he who caused the rocks to be split, the earth to be shaken, the sun to be darkened, the day to flee, the veil of the temple to be divided into two parts? He did not miss it either on the cross, or in death, or in the grave, or in the underworld. Nor is it otherwise, or about another, what is said in the psalm: Remove your gates, princes, and lift them up, eternal gates, and the king of glory will come in. (Ps. 23:7).

VI. Wherefore to those who fear and ask, Who is this king of glory (Ibid., 8)? it will be answered, The Lord is strong and mighty, The Lord is mighty in battle, In which battle, if not in which he trampled death with death, He extinguished sin by killing the innocent, and took back the trophy of victory from the devil and his angels? see what follows: Far, he says, from my salvation are the words of transgressors. You were saddened by this, because I said, I am going to my Father, and you will see me no more (John 16:6); and, if you love me, you will rejoice; because he goes to the Father, because the Father is greater than me (John 14:28). In what, then, does he command his disciples to rejoice? He had come to strengthen us, bearing in himself all kinds of our infirmity. For we have no priest who cannot sympathize with our infirmities (Hebrews 4:15). Father, if it is possible, let this cup pass from me: indeed, not what I will, but what you will (Matthew 26:39). Did he not come to this, that he might drink this cup for us, and the poison thrown by the serpent to such an antidote of salvation did he not have the power to lay down his life, and did he have the power to take it up again (John 10:18)? Did he not himself say: No one takes it from me, but I lay it down of myself (Ibid.)? And yet now as if doubting he speaks and refusing: so that even there the divine power may appear, and here the human condition may know itself. Does he not cry out that this mystery was hidden in God before eternal times? The Apostle (Col. 1, 26)? Did he arrange to be done in eternity with the Father? When these and such things are said or done, as has often been said, they show the true weakness and fragility of man, and do not therefore void the presence of the divine majesty. separated, you will not remember him faithfully promising his presence to the suffering disciples, who say: When they have betrayed you, do not think how or what to speak; for it will be given to you in that hour what to speak. For it is not you who speak, but the spirit of your Father who speaks in you (Matthew 10:19,20). in which, with no existing sin, for our salvation he suffered a harmless death, that he might do the Father's will, denied divine help to himself in the time of the flesh? He allows himself to meditate on something, and he leaves himself on the cross? For he is himself, which must be repeated often and always: neither can the person of God and man be distinguished, although there is a different substance in him. He feared neither to grow perfect, nor to suffer impassive, nor to die immortal, without any change or corruption of himself, as has already been said. received, he lifted him thither from whence he himself had never departed. Let us hear the apostle preaching Christ crucified, indeed a stumbling block to the Jews, but foolishness to the Gentiles: but to those who are called Jews and Greeks, the same Christ. The power of God and the wisdom of God (1 Cor. 1, 23, 24) Take notice, beloved children, and recognize what you already know: Christ himself, who is said to have been a stumbling block to the Jews because of the humility of the man he received, but foolishness to the Gentiles, is himself the power of God and the wisdom of God. or was he ashamed to say the same wisdom of God, which he had called the foolishness of the Gentiles? or to affirm the same power of God, which he had called the offense of the Jews? when do we not deny, by giving to God, that he was made the very man God? Which, of course, is known to have been received by divine grace, not by human substance. sanctification and redemption: as it is written: He that gloryeth, let him glory in the Lord (Ibid., 30, 31). Surely Christ Jesus is only the name of a man, says the heretic. he had known not only man, but also God; which wisdom and justice and sanctification and redemption he believed to have been wrought for us by God; and he taught those who believed in him to glory, because Christ Jesus is both man and God.

VIII. And lest the unjust people of the Jews should claim that they had admitted a small sin, if they understood themselves only as a naked man persecuted; He says the mystery is hidden in the wisdom of God, testifying that it has not been revealed to any of the princes of this world (Ibid., 7, 8). That if they had known, they would never have crucified the Lord of glory. Behold, this Christ Jesus, whom he confesses as Lord of glory, is not afraid to preach himself crucified to the princes of the world. I exhort you to consider the continence of this lesson; and you will see with how much effort and effort the holy apostle raises men's minds from the lowliness of only earthly intelligence to consider the divine in this mystery and heavenly things. In a certain place he speaks thus: If, he says, we have gone beyond God in mind; whether we are temperate, for you: for charity compels us: judging this, that one died for all. reconciling to himself (Ibid., 18, 19).

IX. I ask how: not otherwise than by being born, suffering, dying, rising and ascending to heaven? I also ask what is the mystery of our reconciliation? Christ? Let us see, then, whether man alone has made it perfect: since, as they think, God departed from him in passion. To Christ, reconciling the world to himself. Reconciling in such a way? Not imputing to them their transgressions. Or perhaps this pleases the fools, that the remission of sins should only be effected through a man? That when even the Jews repulsed by saying: He blasphemes: who can forgive sins but God alone (Mark 2 :7)? The Lord himself, the Son of God and man, wanting to make it clear to unbelievers that it was not only man whom they saw, but also God in whom they despised to believe, and to clearly show the divine power contributed to man also because of the unity of his person and presence: That you may know, he says, because the Son of Man has power to forgive sins on earth, then he said to the paralytic: Arise, take up your bed and go to your house (Matthew 9:6). and he lifted the burden of sin within. Therefore, God was in Christ reconciling the world to himself: never and never forsaking man, whom he received of his own condescension, without any necessity at all. The Son, whom he appointed heir of the universe, through whom he made the ages.

X. The Son of God and the Son of man are one and the same, who, because of eternity with the Father, made the ages; he made the cleansing of our sins; and he has a proper reward, he sits at the right hand of the Father. But how did he make the cleansing of sins, except by erasing the writing that had been against us (Col. 2, 14), written by the devil as an accuser? Once God spoke to the fathers in the prophets, and finally testified in the Son (Hebrews 1, 1, 2), let us believe this, let us hold to this, let us defend this with all our strength. himself (Col. 2, 15). That the work is not entirely of man alone, but of the majesty of God in man. For man is not strong and powerful, but the Lord is mighty in war (Ps. 23:6).

XI. Also there after much, to which the apostle distinguished the mystery of the New Testament from the figure of the Old, thus saying: Refusing the law of Moses, he dies without mercy in two or three witnesses: how much more does he seem worthy of a worse punishment who trampled on the Son of God, and who esteemed impure the blood of the New Testament, in which he was sanctified, and he insulted the spirit of God's grace? For we know he who said: Vengeance is mine, I will repay, says the Lord (Heb. 10, 28-30). I ask how God the Son of God can be trampled upon. nor should he be ashamed to assert that the Son of God has been trampled upon. for the Son of God is trampled upon, unless the benefit of the death which he endured in man is spurned. the different opinions of others would suggest to him: But you, he said, who do you say that I am (Ibid., 15)? I am indeed the son of man. To these things Peter, inspired by the same, and in this confession to the right form of his faith, will benefit all the nations, notice how much and with what full integrity he answered: You are the Christ, the Son of the living God (Matthew 16:16). to the apostles, the one substance of both is pointed out and the person is shown; while he also proclaimed himself the son of man, which was seen in the open, and Peter showed him the Christ, the Son of God, which was carried on in secret, by the confession given to him? Whence was he praised by the Lord and called blessed (Ibid., 17); for it was not flesh and blood that revealed it to him, but the Father who is in heaven. What we must believe, then, is that God the Father reveals through God the Son, and not flesh and blood insinuates.

XII. would open the way for him to be recognized and prevent him from doing what he wanted to touch himself; Let us hear what he has designed to delegate to his disciples. to my God and to your God (John 20:17). Go now, let the heretic choose whether he thinks it is, and whose voice he prefers to be, let him judge both sides will be struck with a sharp spiritual sword. I ascend, he says, to my Father and to my father of you to my God, and to your God. If it is the voice of a man, then that man is the Son of God: to my Father, he said, I ascend. If it is the voice of God, then that God is a man: for he said to my God, I ascend. he says, I ascend to my Father, and the God of my man; or, I ascend to my God, and to the Father of my God. Whoever, therefore, discerns the person of divinity and humanity, is convinced of both understandings. Either man said, and he is the same Son of God: or God said, and the same man is also taken up. For he who says, I ascend to my Father and to my God; by repeating mine and mine, he proves and promises one person, although he distinguishes both substances. For what he says, I ascend to my Father, seems indeed to belong to the only begotten Son; but what he says, to my God, seems to belong to the man made. But in Christ Jesus neither man can be said to be created, nor can the only-begotten God be denied, man begotten. And therefore, it is convinced that this voice is neither of God alone, nor of man alone: which God and man, the one and only Son, commanded to bear his disciples with an absolutely inseparable and indivisible affection. Finally, that you may know and be more fully aware that this is what is said, in order to dissolve the devices of all heretics and to refute all slanders; where it was necessary to distinguish the nature of the creator from the creature, see how the divine mercy watched for us. Go, he says, to my brothers and say to them: I ascend to my Father and to your Father; to my God and to your God. Here it is evident that the person of the Lord, that is, of God and man, is distinguished from the person of his servants, and the calling is separated from nature. for he could say, I ascend to our Father and to our God; for there is a great distance between dominion and condition, between generation and adoption, between substance and grace. Therefore, it is not here mixed up or scattered that it is said, I ascend to our Father and to our God: but to my Father and your father, to my God and to your God for God is a father to him in a different way, to us in a different way. If nature makes him equal, mercy humbles him: but nature prostrates us, mercy raises us up.

XIII. And who will be able, or to whom it is sufficient in the holy pages, to gather together all the documents at one time, by which these sincere and mere truths will be taught? I acknowledged it. Immediately, therefore, as the Apostle commanded (II Tim. 4:2), in a timely and importunate manner; and sound doctrine reprove, recall, instruct, strengthen all who are wandering: not mine, which are none or little, having proofs in this rule of faith; but of the divine Scriptures, and of great and learned men, who held these things before us most firmly, and taught them most eloquently in many books.

LATIN TEXT

EPISTOLA PRIMA. AD CONCILIUM EPHESINUM.

De una Christi Dei et hominis persona adversus Nestorium. I. Optabam, piissimi fratres, venerandam vestram synodum in tali rerum statu congregatam fuisse, quo nobis quoque, delectis communi sententia aliquot ex fratribus et coepiscopis nostris, instructam potius legationem mittere licuisset, quam excusationem lamentatione dignam; nisi hanc animi nostri affectionem diversae causae impedivissent. Primum enim domini et filii nostri religiosissimi Theodosii imperatoris litterae ad manus nostras perlatae, ejusmodi erant, quae beatae memoriae fratris et coepiscopi nostri Augustini praesentiam peculiari ratione efflagitabant. Verum cum eae litterae illum jam tum e vivis excessisse comperissent, ego regiam illam significationem, licet ad praedictum Augustinum praecipue destinata videretur, excipiens, missis ad universas Africae provincias congruis litteris consuetisque sermonibus, synodum cogere volui convenientem; quo nimirum ex fratrum et episcoporum nostrorum numero seligerentur nonnulli, qui ad venerabilem beatitudinis vestrae synodum destinarentur. At omnis hac tempestate viae aditus praeclusus est. Etenim effusa hostium multitudo, et ingens ubique provinciarum vastatio, quae incolis partim exstinctis, partim in fugam actis, miseram desolationis speciem, quoquoversum longe lateque porrigitur, oculis offert, promptam illam veniendi facultatem reprimit. His itaque impedimentis episcopi quibus propositum id erat, prohibiti, ex Africae ambitu simul convenire nequiverunt. Hisce incommodis accedebat, litteras imperatoris in diebus paschae ad nos perlatas esse, quando jam inde usque ad universalem venerandam synodum vix duorum mensium spatium supererat. Quod sane temporis intervallum, etsi nulla impraesentiarum ab hostibus difficultas fuisset objecta, vel ad Africanam synodum cogendam vix satis erat. Hinc factum est, ut licet solemnem aliquam legationem mittere nequaquam voluerimus, attamen propter reverentiam et observantiam quae ecclesiasticae disciplinae debetur, filium meum Besulam diaconum una cum his excusationis litteris ad vos, venerabiles fratres, destinaverimus. II. Quamobrem vestram sanctitatem iterum atque iterum rogatam cupio (etiamsi fidem catholicam per tantam venerandorum sacerdotum synodum, Dei nostri auxilio in omnibus stabilem ac firmam futuram certo confidam) ut Spiritu sancto cooperante, quem cordibus vestris in omnibus quae acturi estis, praesto futurum non dubito, novas doctrinas, et antehac ecclesiasticis auribus inusitatas, priscae auctoritatis robore instructi e medio profligetis, atque ita quibuscunque novis erroribus resistatis; ne hos quos pridem impugnavit Ecclesia, hisque temporibus repullulantes, apostolicae sedis auctoritas, sacerdotumque in unum consonans sententia oppressit, secundae disputationis praetextu vox jam dudum ablata renovare videatur. Nam si quid forte novarum controversiarum inciderit, id discussioni subjiciatur oportet: ut vel recte dictum comprobetur, vel condemnatione dignum explodatur. At vero si quis ea quae jam olim dijudicata sunt, denuo in disputationem vocari sinat; is sane aliud nihil facere censebitur, quam de fide quae hactenus valuit, ipsemet dubitare. Deinde ad posteritatis exemplum, ut ea quae nunc pro catholica fide definita sunt, perpetuam firmitatem obtinere valeant; oportet ea omnia inconcussa immotaque conservare, quae superioribus temporibus a sanctis Patribus constituta sunt. Nam qui illam perpetuam stabilitatem retinere voluerit quae de catholicae fidei ratione statuerit, is non propria auctoritate, sed antiquorum Patrum judicio sententiam suam corroborare debet: ita ut ea ratione partim veterum, partim recentiorum decretis et sententiis placita sua comprobans, unicam Ecclesiae veritatem jam inde ab initio ad praesens usque tempus simplici puritate invictaque constantia et auctoritate decurrentem, se asserere, docere et tenere ostendat. Haec pro praesenti Africanorum legatione, quam necessitas superius memorata impedivit, venerabilibus vestris auribus suggerere volui; obnixe interim rogans, ut calamitatibus rerum praesentiumque temporum spectatis, nostram absentiam non superbiae aut negligentiae, sed manifestae huic necessitati ascribere velitis. Cyrillus Ecclesiae Alexandrinae episcopus dixit: Et haec reverendissimi piissimique Carthaginis episcopi Capreoli quae lecta est epistola, cum dilucidam sententiam in se contineat, fidei gestorum inseratur. Vult enim antiqua fidei dogmata confirmari, nova vero et absurde excogitata et impie divulgata reprobari ac proscribi.

Omnes episcopi simul exclamaverunt: Hae omnium voces: haec omnes asserimus: hoc omnium est votum.

Ηὐχόμην, εὐλαβέστατοι ἀδελφοί, ἐν τοιαύτῃ καταστάσει τὴν προσκυνητὴν ὑμῶν σύνοδον συγκροτηθῆναι, ἵνα καὶ ἡμεῖς, ἐπιλεχθέντων κοινῇ κρίσει ἀδελφῶν καὶ συνεπισκόπων ἡμετέρων, οὐ παραίτησιν θρήνου ἀξίαν, ἀλλὰ παρεσκευασμένην μᾶλλον πρεσβείαν πέμψωμεν· εἰ μὴ τὴν ἡμετέραν σύστασιν αἰτίαι διάφοροι ἐνεπόδιζον. Καὶ γὰρ πρῶτον τοῦ δεσπότου καὶ υἱοῦ ἡμετέρου τοῦ εὐσεβεστάτου βασιλέως Θεοδοσίου τοιαῦτα εἰς τὰς ἡμετέρας χεῖρας γράμματα ἐλήλυθεν, ἅ τινα τοῦ τῆς μακαρίας μνήμης ἀδελφοῦ ἡμετέρου καὶ συνεπισκόπου Αὐγουστίνου τὴν παρουσίαν ἰδικῶς ἀπῄτει· ἅ τινα προειρημένα γράμματα εἰς ταύτην τὴν ζωὴν εὑρεῖν αὐτὸν οὐδαμῶς δεδύνηνται. Ὅθεν ἐγὼ, ὅς τις τὴν αὐτὴν βασιλικὴν σημείωσιν, εἰ καὶ τὰ μάλιστα τῷ προειρημένῳ πεπέμφθαι ἐδόκει, ἐδεξάμην καταπεμφθεῖσαν, κατὰ πάσας τὰς ἐπαρχίας τῆς Ἀφρικῆς τοῖς ἁρμοδίοις γράμμασι, καὶ ταῖς ἐθίμοις διαλέξεσι συνάδουσαν σύνοδον ἠβουλήθην συναγαγεῖν, ἵνα ἐπιλεχθέντες ἀπὸ τοῦ ἀριθμοῦ τῶν ἀδελφῶν καὶ ἐπισκόπων τῶν ἡμετέρων εἰς τὴν προσκυνητὴν σύνοδον τῆς ὑμετέρας μακαριότητος καταπεμφθῶσιν. Ἀλλ' ἐπειδὴ οὐκ ἀνέῳκται ἡ εἴσοδος τῆς παροδίας· καὶ γὰρ ἡ ἐπιχυθεῖσα πολεμία πληθὺς, καὶ ἡ πόρθησις ἡ πλατεῖα τῶν ἐπαρχιῶν, ἤ τις ἡ ἀποσβεσθέντων τῶν οἰκητόρων, ἢ φυγόντων, ἀθλίαν ἐρημώσεως ὄψιν εἰς μῆκος καὶ πλάτος ἐκτείνουσα, τὴν εὐχέρειαν συστέλλει τοῦ ἐλθεῖν. Τούτοις τοιγαροῦν τοῖς κωλύμασι συνελθεῖν εἰς ἓν τοῦ κύκλου τῆς Ἀφρικῆς οἱ ἐπίσκοποι οὐδαμῶς ἠδυνήθησαν, οἷς προετέθη. Ἐπειδὴ τὰ βασιλικὰ γράμματα ἐν ἡμέραις τοῦ πάσχα εἰς ἡμᾶς ἦλθε, ὅτε μόλις μέχρι τῆς πρόσκυνητῆς πάσης συνόδου δύο μηνῶν διάστημα περιελιμπάνετο οἵ τινες μόλις ἤρκουν, κἂν αὐτῇ τῇ κατὰ Ἀφρικὴν συνόδῳ εἰς τὸ συνελθεῖν, καὶ εἰ μηδεμία δυσχέρεια ἀπὸ τῶν πολεμίων ἡ παροῦσα συμβεβήκει ἐντεῦθεν γεγενῆσθαι· ἵνα, εἰ καὶ τὰ μάλιστα πρέσβεις οὐδαμῶς ἐκπέμψαι δεδυνήμεθα, διὰ τὴν εὐλάβειαν ὅμως τὴν χρεωστουμένην τῇ ἐκκλησιαστικῇ ἐπιστήμῃ, τὸν υἱὸν τὸν ἐμὸν Βεσούλαν τὸν διάκονον μετὰ τούτων τῶν τῆς παραιτήσεως γραμμάτων ἐπέμψαμεν, προσκυνητοὶ ἀδελφοί.

Ὅθεν αἰτῶ τὴν ὑμετέραν ἁγιότητα· εἰ καὶ τὰ μάλιστα πιστεύω τῇ βοηθείᾳ τοῦ ἡμετέρου Θεοῦ, τοσαύτην σύνοδον προσκυνητῶν ἱερέων βεβαίαν διὰ πάντων τὴν πίστιν τὴν καθολικὴν ἐσομένην· ἵνα, ἐνεργοῦντος τοῦ ἁγίου πνεύματος, ὅπερ ταῖς ὑμετέραις καρδίαις ἐν πᾶσι τοῖς πρακτέοις πιστεύομεν παρεσόμενον, τὰς καινὰς διδασκαλίας, καὶ πρὸ τούτου ταῖς ἐκκλησιαστικαῖς ἀκοαῖς ἀπείρους, τῆς ἀρχαίας αὐθεντίας τῇ δυνάμει ἀπώσησθε, καὶ οὕτω ταῖς καιναῖς οἱαισδήποτε πλάναις ἀντιστῆτε· ἵνα μὴ τούτους, οὓς πάλαι ἐπολέμησεν ἡ ἐκκλησία, καὶ τούτοις τοῖς καιροῖς ἐν οἷς ἀνεφύησαν, καὶ τῆς ἀποστολικῆς καθέδρας ἡ αὐθεντία, καὶ εἰς ἓν συμφωνοῦσα ἡ ψῆφος ἡ ἱερατικὴ συνέχωσεν, ἐν προσχήματι δευτέρας διαλέξεως ἡ φωνὴ δόξῃ, ἡ πάλαι ἀναιρεθεῖσα, ἀνανεοῦσθαι. Ἔχει γὰρ, εἴ τι τυχὸν νεωστὶ ἀναφυῇ, ζητήσεως ἀνάγκην, ἵνα ἢ λεχθὲν δοκιμασθῇ, ἢ καταδικασθὲν δυνηθῇ ἀποκρουσθῆναι. Ταῦτα δὲ περὶ ὧν ἤδη πάλαι ἐκρίθη ἐάν τις ἐπαφῇ εἰς δευτέραν διάλεξιν κληθῆναι, οὐδὲν ἕτερον δόξει, ἢ περὶ τῆς πίστεως, ἢ τις μέχρι δεῦρο κατέσχεν, αὐτὸς ἀμφιβάλλειν. Ἔπειτα διὰ τὸ τῶν μεταγενεστέρων ὑπόδειγμα· ἵνα ταῦτα ἅπερ νῦν ὑπὲρ τῆς καθολικῆς πίστεως ὥρισται, ἔχειν δυνηθῇ διηνεκῆ βεβαίωσιν, ταῦτα ἅπερ ἤδη ἐστὶ παρὰ τῶν πατέρων ὁρισθέντα, φυλακτέα ἐστίν. Ἐπειδὴ ὅστις βούλεται, ἅπερ ὑπὲρ τῆς καθολικῆς καταστάσεως ἐθέσπισεν, εἰς τὸ διηνεκὲς μένειν, οὐ τῇ ἰδίᾳ αὐθεντίᾳ, ἀλλὰ καὶ τῇ τῶν ἀρχαιοτέρων ψήφῳ ὀφείλει βεβαιωθῆναι ὅπερ ἐφρόνησεν· ὥστε οὕτως τοῦτο μὲν ἀπὸ τῶν ἀρχαιοτέρων, τοῦτο δὲ καὶ ἀπὸ νεωτέρων ὅρων, ὅπερ διαβεβαιοῦται, δοκιμάζων, μονογενῆ τῆς καθολικῆς ἐκκλησίας τὴν ἀλήθειαν, ἀπὸ τῶν παρῳχημένων καιρῶν μέχρι τῶν παρόντων ἤτοι τῶν ἡμετέρων, ἁπλῇ καθαρότητι, καὶ ἀηττήτῳ αὐθεντίᾳ τρέχουσαν. ἑαυτὸν καὶ λέγειν, καὶ διδάξειν, καὶ κατέχειν. Ταῦτα τέως ὑπὲρ τῆς παρούσης πρεσβείας τῆς Ἀφρικῆς, ἥν τινα καταπέμψαι ἡ ἀνάγκη ἡ προρρηθεῖσα οὐ συνεχώρησε, ταῖς προσκυνηταῖς ὑμῶν ἀκοαῖς ὑπέβαλον, πλεῖστα παρακαλῶν, ἵνα θεωρηθεισῶν τῶν ἐν τοῖς πράγμασι καὶ τοῖς καιροῖς συμφορῶν, τὴν ἡμετέραν ἀπουσίαν μηδεμίᾳ ὑπερηφανίᾳ ἢ ἀμελείᾳ ἀλλὰ ταύτῃ τῇ προδήλῳ ἀνάγκῃ μᾶλλον λογίσασθαι καταξιώσητε.

Κύριλλος ἐπίσκοπος Ἀλεξανδρείας εἶπε· Καὶ ἡ ἀναγνωσθεῖσα ἐπιστολὴ τοῦ εὐλαβεστάτου καὶ θεοφιλεστάτου ἐπισκόπου τῆς Καρθαγένης Καπραϊόλου ἐμφερέσθω τῇ πίστει τῶν ὑπομνημάτων, φανερὰν ἔχουσα διάνοιαν. Βούλεται γὰρ, τὰ μὲν ἀρχαῖα κρατύνεσθαι τῆς πίστεως δόγματα, τὰ δὲ νεαρὰ, καὶ ἀτόπως ἐξευρημένα. καὶ ἀσεβῶς εἰρημένα, ἀποδοκιμάζεσθαι καὶ ἐκβάλλεσθαι.

Πάντες οἱ ἐπίσκοποι ἀνεφώνησαν· αὗται πάντων αἱ φωναί· ταῦτα πάντες λέγομεν· αὕτη πάντων ἡ εὐχή.

EPISTOLA SERVORUM DEI VITALIS ET CONSTANTII SPANORUM AD S. CAPREOLUM EPISCOPUM ECCLESIAE CATHOLICAE CARTHAGINIS.

Domino et venerabili et beatissimo in Christo famulo Dei, domino nostro Capreolo, Vitalis et Constantius peccatores.

Quae prima vota sunt humilitatis nostrae, plurimum salutamus sanctam perfectamque et venerabilem beatitudinem tuam, et sanum atque incolumem semper Deo propitio audire desideramus: quia etsi in longinquo positi sumus a sancto apostolatu vestro, mari terminante, sed in praesentia vestri sumus semper in orationibus sanctitatis vestrae, domine Pater. Illud sane multum desiderii nostri fuit, scribere sanctae honorificentiae tuae per dulcissimum fratrem nostrum Numinianum. Reperit enim parvitas nostra praecellentem famam et doctrinam tuae sanctitatis: per quam et scribimus beatitudini tuae, ut ait Psalmographus: In omnem terram exivit sonus eorum, et in fines orbis terrae verba eorum (Psal. XVIII, 5). Illud etiam consulimus honorificentiam tuam, ut de bono thesauro cordis tui nostris visceribus irrigari jubeas, quae fides catholica recta teneat. Quia sunt hic quidam qui dicunt non debere dici Deum natum. Nam et haec est fides eorum, hominem purum natum fuisse de Maria virgine, et post haec Deum habitasse in eo. Quorum nos humiles pueri tui resistimus affirmationi, non ita debere dici: sed confitemur, ut ait evangelista, annuntiante angelo Gabriele Mariae dicente: Spiritus sanctus veniet in te, et virtus Altissimi obumbrabit tibi: ideoque quod nascetur ex te sanctum, vocabitur Filius Dei (Luc. I, 35).

II. Confitemur itaque Deum fuisse in utero Mariae virginis, assumpsisse aliquam partem, fabricasse Deum sibi hominem, natum fuisse Deum verum et hominem verum quem assumpsit pro salute generis humani, ut ait Apostolus: Cum venit plenitudo temporis, misit Deus Filium suum factum ex muliere, factum sub lege, ut eos qui sub lege erant redimeret (Gal. IV, 4). Et iterum: Hoc autem sentite in vobis, quod et in Christo Jesu: qui cum in forma Dei esset, non rapinam arbitratus est esse aequalis Deo: sed semetipsum exinanivit formam servi accipiens, in similitudinem hominum factus, et habitu inventus ut homo. Humiliavit semetipsum factus obediens usque ad mortem, mortem autem crucis (Philip. II, 5-8). Et iterum: Mediator Dei et hominum, homo Christus Jesus (I Tim. II, 5). Quia mediator nec jam Deus tantum pure sine homine quem assumpsit dici potest, nec homo sine Deo: quia duplex in una persona mediatoris significatio, Deus et homo: dum Deus de Deo Deus, et secundum carnem idem ipse filius hominis. Ideo verus

Deus et homo verus est hic mediator, sicut de forma Dei et forma hominis. Nam et in principio inchoationis ad Romanos sic dicit sanctus Apostolus: Quod ante promiserat per prophetas suos in Scripturis sanctis de Filio suo, qui factus est ei ex semine David secundum carnem: qui praedestinatus est Filius Dei in virtute secundum spiritum sanctificationis, ex resurrectione mortuorum, Jesu Christi Domini nostri (Rom. I, 2-4). Verum etiam et Isaias auctor prophetarum sic dicit: Ecce virgo in utero concipiet, et pariet filium, et vocabitis nomen ejus Emmanuel, quod est interpretatum, Nobiscum Deus (Isai. VII, 14; Matth. I, 23). Sed et hominem purum dicunt pependisse in cruce comprehensum: aiunt, Recessit Deus ab eo. Quibus parvitas nostra sic dicit, Nunquam Deus recessit ab homine assumpto, nisi quando dixit de cruce: Heli, Heli, Lammasabactani: Deus, Deus meus, quare me dereliquisti (Matth. XXVII, 46)? Ideoque provoluti genibus exoramus humiles servi tui sanctum apostolatum vestrum, ut informetis parvitatem nostram in his quod rectum habet fides catholica: et detis veniam insipientiae vel imperitiae nostrae, si quid per ignorantiam incedimus. Potens est Dominus Christus sanctis orationibus vestris nobis veniam dare, ne deveniamus in profundum malorum. Ora pro nobis, domine sancte, venerabilis et beatissime papa. SUBSCRIPTIO. Incolumem venerabilitatem tuam nobis Dominus noster Jesus longiorem conservet, domine sancte ac venerabilis papa.

EPISTOLA II SEU RESCRIPTUM AD VITALEM ET CONSTANTIUM. De una Christi veri Dei et hominis persona, contra recens damnatam haeresim Nestorii.

Dilectissimis et religiosis filiis Vitali et Constantio Capreolus episcopus. I. Sumptis atque perlectis litteris vestris, quas per Numinianum religiosum virum, filii dilectissimi, transmisistis, saluti et studio vestro quo fundatae ac vetustae catholicae fidei regulam inviolabili pietate tenetis ac defenditis, plurimum gratulatus, adverti Nestorianam haeresim, novam infandamque perniciem, sicut quibusdam locis jam coeperat pullulare, apud vos quoque velle zizaniae suae semina in peritorum corda jacere. Verum credo atque confido, perfectum agricolam Dominum nostrum, omnium creatorem, in omni loco dominationis suae habere ac semper habuisse dignos evangelicae frugis operarios; qui, licet ante tempus demessionis immunda semina exstirpari non debeant, continuis tamen orationibus ac praedicationibus semper invigilent: ita ut et illa, si fieri dum tempus est potuerit, convertantur et commutentur in triticum: aut certe non usquequaque inimicus humani generis tenera frumentorum genera nascentia per adulterinam intermixtionem valeat suffocare. Jam enim, quod etiam ad vestram notitiam pervenisse non dubito, intra Orientis partes, ubi primum pestis ista surrexit, congregata gloriosa synodo sacerdotum, cui etiam legatio nostra non defuit in vestibulo cum suo auctore atque assertore compressa et radio apostolicae lucis exstincta est. Nec mirari debet caritas vestra, si etiam post damnationem suam inter morientes spiritus fetidus adhuc flatus aspiret. Est enim semper pertinax haereticorum audacia, et in sua male pernicie urgente peccatorum pondere perseverat. Quod si nondum forsitan cognovistis, facili lectione poteritis agnoscere.

II. Quamvis igitur Christianis et devotis mentibus ipsa universalis Ecclesiae auctoritas plene sufficiat, nec vestra, quantum missus a vobis sermo perdocuit, in hac causa minor videatur assertio: ne tamen ego quoque petitioni atque interrogationi sanctae necessarium videar negare responsum, unam veramque doctrinam hanc esse confitemur, quam evangelica tenet ac tradit antiquitas. Id est: Dei Filium, Deum verum, et hominem verum, unius prorsus atque inseparabilis esse personae: nec sicut in aliis patriarchis, prophetis, apostolis, caeterisque sanctis et praeclarissimis viris habitavit aut habitat Deus, ita in Christum Jesum divinam illam plenitudinem velut extrinsecus credimus advenisse; sed proprio quodam atque ineffabili modo, Filium Dei etiam filium hominis factum: ut qui ingenita Patris substantia unigenitus permanebat ac permanet, mirabiliter suscepto homine, fieret primogenitus in multis fratribus (Rom. VIII, 29): et qui erat in principio Verbum, et Verbum erat apud Deum, et Deus erat Verbum, Verbum caro fieret et habitaret in nobis (Joan. I, 1, 14). Ex quo igitur mysterium quod absconditum fuit a saeculis (Col. I, 26) in Deo, coepit per angelum in utero virginis operari, atque in ea sanctus Spiritus supervenit, et illi virtus Altissimi obumbravit (Luc. I, 35); Deus in homine nasci dignatus est, qui semper erat, ut homo nasceretur, qualis ante non fuerat. Qui enim sine matre in coelis aeterne genitus, ipse in terris sine patre in utero virginis homo de Spiritu sancto creatus est. Et ideo in Christo Jesu separari vel subdividi Dei hominisque nullo modo credimus posse personam: ne non jam in divinitate Trinitas, sed quaternitas numeretur. III. Beatus apostolus Paulus dum ad exuendum veterem hominem et induendum novum fideles exhortaretur: Primus, inquit, homo de terra terrenus, secundus homo de coelo coelestis: qualis terrenus, tales et terreni; et qualis coelestis, tales et coelestes: quomodo portavimus imaginem terreni, portemus et imaginem ejus qui de coelo est (I Cor. XV, 47-49). Rogo dicant, quomodo est homo iste de coelo, si non est Deus conceptus in utero? aut quae discretio est carnis et sanguinis in homine Adam, et in homine Christo, si non homo iste plenus est Deo? Quid enim sibi vult secundus homo de coelo? Nunquid caro transmissa descendit, ac non, sicut scriptum est, Spiritus sanctus in virginem supervenit? Sed quia Verbum caro factum est (Joan. I, 14), ideo coelestis homo appellatus est. Nec propterea carnem veram non habuit, quia de coelo descendit; quia carnem Deus accepit. Merito de se ipso idem Dominus dixit: Nemo ascendit in coelum, nisi qui de coelo descendit, filius hominis qui est in coelo (Joan. III, 13). Certe adhuc loquebatur in terra, nec ad Patrem post victoriam passionis et gloriam resurrectionis ascenderat: et tamen filium hominis jam in coelo esse dicebat. Hoc utique omni veritate testificans, quia et propter hominem Deus conversabatur in terra, et propter Deum homo habitabat in coelo. Unde etiam Apostolus: Qui descendit, inquit, ipse est et qui ascendit super omnes coelos, ut adimpleret omnia (Ephes. IV, 10). Item alibi, cum de carnis suae cibo et potu sanguinis Salvator ipse mystice loqueretur, sciens quod offensi ex hoc ejus discipuli murmurarent dicentes: Durus est hic sermo, quis potest eum audire (Joan. VI, 61)? sic ait: Hoc vos scandalizat? Si ergo videritis filium hominis ascendentem ubi erat prius (Ibid., 63)? Ecce et hic advertitis quemadmodum propter unitatem Dei hominisque personae, filium hominis ubi erat prius perhibet ascensurum, quem in utero virginis constat esse formatum, ut ex eo humanae nativitatis sumpsisset principium. IV. Nemo itaque sacrilego spiritu audeat separare quod videt in coelo et in terra unitate inseparabili permanere. Sicut enim ab omnipotentia Deitatis homo Christus Jesus esse non potest alienus; ita et ab his quae in hominem vel circa hominem gesta sunt, separari non potest Deus. Natus ergo est homo qui nondum fuerat, quia Verbum caro factum est, et inhabitavit in nobis (Joan. I, 14). Simili modo passus est impassibilis per passibilem quem suscepit, et immortalis mortuus est, et qui nunquam moritur resurrexit. Neque enim vel in passione defuit illi homini Deus: alioquin non est Dominus gloriae crucifixus (I Cor. II, 8). An dicimus Deum in suscepto homine etiam apud inferos non fuisse? aut vero metuendum est, ne divinitas ibi quasi poenaliter fuerit, quam nulla qualitas afficit, nulla demensio circumscribit? cujus magnitudinem nemo capit, praesentiam nemo fugit, secretum nemo invenit, splendorem nullus attingit? Times includi immensum? teneri omnipotentem? abscondi ubicunque diffusum? Resolvere, sicut scriptum est, inferorum parturitiones, in quibus voluit et qualiter voluit rerum Dominus, subjici hujusmodi conditioni non potuit (Act. II, 24). Audi eum ante tot annorum millia, dum beato Job mirabilium suorum opera per nubem velut improperanti similis praedicaret, hoc quoque inter innumeras sui potentias cumulantem: Nunquid tu abstulisti impiis lucem, aut brachium superborum comminuisti? aut venisti ad fines maris? aut in vestigiis abyssi ambulasti? aut tibi, inquit, aperientur metu portae mortis, aut janitores inferni videntes te timuerunt? aut cognovisti latitudinem sub coelo (Job XXXVIII, 15-18, sec. LXX)? Si Patris haec vox est, nihil ergo est omnipotenti difficile, quoniam ubique est, nusquam non est. Quando ei etiam propheta ex persona cujusdam dicit: Quo ibo a spiritu tuo, et a facie tua quo fugiam? si ascendero in coelum, tu ibi es; si descendero in infernum, ades (Psal. CXXXVIII, 7, 8). Hoc omnino testificans ac demonstrans, Deum cujus majestate plena sunt omnia, quodam incomprehensibili utique et inexplicabili modo etiam inferis interesse. Si autem, quod magis probabile est, in his quae de eo tanto ante in prophetia praedicta sunt, et impleta Filii Dei vox est, quoniam per ipsum facta sunt omnia, et sine ipso factum est nihil (Joan. I, 3): ipse in homine est visitare inferorum dignatus obstrusa, et praepositos mortis praesentia invictae majestatis exterruit, et propter liberandos quos voluit, inferorum portas reserari praecepit. V. De ipso siquidem Joannes apostolus in Apocalypsi sic loquitur: Posuit manum dexteram super me dicens: Noli timere: ego sum primus et novissimus; et vivens, qui fueram mortuus; et ecce sum vivens in saecula saeculorum: et habeo clavem mortis et inferorum (Apoc. I, 17, 18). Propter deitatem quippe primus, quoniam principium est quod et loquitur nobis (Joan. VIII, 25): propter humanitatem vero novissimus, quia suscipere crucem non dedignatus est et mortem pro nobis. Et ideo cui in Divinitate nuda sunt omnia creaturarum, etiam in homine suscepto habet claves mortis et inferorum. Tantum igitur abest, Deum Dei Filium, incommutabilem atque incomprehensibilem, ab inferis potuisse concludi; ut nec ipsam assumptionis animam credamus, aut exitiabiliter susceptam, aut tenaciter derelictam. Sed nec carnem ejus credimus contagione alicujus corruptionis infectam. Ipsius namque vox est in psalmo, sicut Petrus interpretatur apostolus: Non derelinques animam meam apud inferos, neque sanctum tuum videre corruptionem (Psal. XV, 10; Act. II, 28). Ipse propter culpam nostram factus est velut homo sine adjutorio (Psal. LXXXVII, 6): propter innocentiam vero ac potentiam suam inventus est inter mortuos liber. Tunc enim vere quae non rapuerat, sicut scriptum est (Ps. LXVIII, 5) exsolvebat. Non itaque mirum, si Deum locus aliquis recipit, nec tamen capit: praesentiam sentit, majestatem non impedit: expavescit omnipotentiam, substantiam non includit. Siquidem illa summa et perfecta beatitudo et inexstinguibilis lucis [forte lux], nec obscurari tenebris, nec variari locis, nec passionibus affici, nec conditionibus minui, nec temporibus valeat commutari. Deus ergo filium proprium hominem nec in inferis deseruit, nec apud inferos dereliquit. Cujus autem virtute ac majestate antiqua sanctorum corpora visa sunt resurrexisse (Matth. XXVII, 51, 52), si Deus inferos minime visitavit? Quis ille est qui petras scindi, terram commoveri, solem obscurari, diem fugere, velum templi in duas dividi partes effecit? Nunquid homo tantum? nonne etiam Deus? Ergo ei nec in cruce, nec in morte, nec in sepulcro, nec in inferis defuit. Nec aliter, aut de alio solet intelligi quod in psalmo dictum est: Auferte portas, principes, vestras, et elevamini, portae aeternales, et introibit rex gloriae (Psal. XXIII, 7). Unde expavescentibus atque interrogantibus, Quis est iste rex gloriae (Ibid., 8)? respondetur, Dominus fortis et potens, Dominus potens in praelio, Quo praelio, nisi in quo mortem morte calcavit, peccatum innocens occisus exstinxit, et tropaeum victoriae de diabolo et angelis ejus reportavit? VI. At enim ipse in cruce dixit: Deus, Deus meus, quare me dereliquisti (Psal. XXI, 1)? Sed ista suscepti hominis vox est. Attende unde assumpta est, et illic vide quid sequitur: Longe, inquit, a salute mea verba delictorum (Ibid.). Similis est haec vox etiam illi qua dicitur: Tristis est anima mea usque ad mortem (Matth, XXVI, 38).

Nonne paulo ante ipse discipulis dixerat: In hoc contristati estis, quoniam dixi, Eo ad Patrem meum, et jam non videbitis me (Joan. XVI, 6); et, Si diligeretis me, gauderetis; quia eo ad Patrem, quia Pater major me est (Joan. XIV, 28). In quo ergo jubet gaudere discipulos suos? Qualiter creditur contristari magister, nisi ut in homine veri hominis passiones et fluctuationes ostenderet? Qui enim propter nos redimendos, instituendos, confirmandosque venerat, omnia in se infirmitatis nostrae genera sustinebat. Non enim habemus sacerdotem, qui non possit compati infirmitatibus nostris (Hebr. IV, 15): etenim sicut Apostolus ait, Expertus est omnia secundum similitudinem sine peccato. Similis huic est etiam illa vox: Pater, si fieri potest, transeat a me calix iste: verum non quod ego volo, sed quod tu vis (Matth. XXVI, 39). Nonne in hoc venerat, ut pro nobis hunc calicem biberet, et venenum a serpente propinatum tali antidoto salutis expelleret? Nonne potestatem habebat ponendi animam suam, et potestatem habebat iterum sumendi eam (Joan. X, 18)? Nonne ipse dixerat: Nemo tollit eam a me, sed ego a me ipso pono eam (Ibid.)? Et tamen nunc velut dubitans loquitur et recusans: ut et illic divina potestas appareat, et hic se conditio humana cognoscat. Nonne hoc mysterium ante tempora aeterna in Deo fuisse absconditum clamat. Apostolus (Col. I, 26)? Num vero velut repentinum aliquid Christus expavit, quod certo tempore faciendum in aeternitate cum Patre disposuit? Haec ergo et talia cum dicuntur aut fiunt, sicut saepe dictum est, veram hominis infirmitatem fragilitatemque demonstrant, nec ideo praesentiam divinae majestatis evacuant. VII. Hic homo quisquis es, qui putas Deum Christum ab homine Christo passionis tempore separatum, non recordaris eum passuris discipulis suam praesentiam fideliter pollicentem, qui dicit: Cum vos tradiderint, nolite cogitare quomodo aut quid loquamini; dabitur enim vobis in illa hora quid loquamini. Non enim vos estis qui loquimini, sed spiritus Patris vestri qui loquitur in vobis (Matth. X, 19, 20). Itane ille qui servis facientibus Domini voluntatem suam divinam praesentiam promisit, donavit, exhibuit; in quo nullo existente peccato, pro nostra salute mortem subiit innoxiam, ut Patris faceret voluntatem, divinum auxilium sibi carnis tempore denegavit? Et Deus hominem quem ob haec sustinenda nulla compulsus necessitate suscepit, in hac perfunctione destituit? Loquitur inter tormenta martyrum praesens, nec eos aliquid meditari permittit, et se ipsum in crucis patibulo dereliquit? Ipse est enim, quod saepe ac semper est repetendum: nec distingui potest Dei hominisque persona, quamvis sit in eo diversa substantia. Absit aliud credere, absit aliter de omnipotente sentire. Nec nasci aeternus, nec crescere perfectus, nec impassibilis pati, nec immortalis mori, sine ulla sui mutatione vel corruptione, sicut jam dictum est, formidavit. Sed quia haec pati non posset sola Divinitas, hominem per quem tanti muneris mysterio perfungeretur, accepit. Nam et in coelum receptus, illuc eum levavit unde nunquam ipse discessit.

Audiamus Apostolum praedicantem Christum crucifixum, Judaeis quidem scandalum, gentibus autem stultitiam: ipsis vero vocatis Judaeis et Graecis, eumdem ipsum Christum. Dei virtutem et Dei sapientiam (I Cor. I, 23, 24). Advertite, filii dilectissimi, et quod jam nostis agnoscite: ipsum Christum, qui propter humilitatem suscepti hominis Judaeis dicitur fuisse scandalum, gentibus autem stultitia, ipsum esse Dei virtutem et Dei sapientiam. Nunquid vel hic separata aut discreta est ab Apostolo divinitatis humanitatisque persona? aut erubuit eamdem dicere Dei sapientiam, quam factam dixerat gentium stultitiam? aut eumdem asserere Dei virtutem, quem scandalum dixerat Judaeorum? Quid ergo nos erubescimus confiteri Deum propter hominem atque in homine natum et passum; cum non negamus donante Deo factum eumdem ipsum hominem Deum? Quod utique per divinam gratiam, non per humanam substantiam accepisse cognoscitur. VIII. Adhuc paulo infra subsequitur: Ex ipso autem vos estis in Christo Jesu, qui factus est nobis a Deo sapientia et justitia et sanctificatio et redemptio: ut quemadmodum scriptum est: Qui gloriatur, in Domino glorietur (Ibid., 30, 31). Certe Christus Jesus hominis tantum nomen est, ait haereticus. Sed Paulus, qui sciebat et dixerat non esse in homine gloriandum, Christum Jesum non tantum hominem, sed Deum quoque cognoverat; quem sapientiam et justitiam et sanctificationem et redemptionem nobis a Deo factum esse credebat; et in eo credentes gloriari docebat: quoniam Christus Jesus et homo et Deus est. Et ad haec consequenter non elatione verbi aut sapientiae, mysterium Dei annuntians addit et dicit: Nihil me judicavi scire in vobis, nisi Jesum Christum, et hunc crucifixum (I Cor. II, 2). Ac ne Judaeorum iniquus populus parvum se asserat admisisse peccatum, si se intelligat nudum tantum hominem persecutum; mysterium in Dei sapientia dicit absconditum, nulli principum hujus saeculi revelatum testificans (Ibid., 7, 8). Quod si cognovissent, nunquam Dominum gloriae crucifixissent. Ecce et hic Christum Jesum quem Dominum gloriae confitetur, ipsum praedicare non metuit saeculi principibus crucifixum. Omnem hujus lectionis continentiam consideretis exhortor; et videbitis quanto molimine atque conatu, sanctus Apostolus hominum mentes a terrenae tantum intelligentiae vilitate ad divina in hoc mysterio et coelestia consideranda sustollat. Breviter enim cuncta transeo, quae ipsi plenius et latius poteritis advertere. Nam et ad Corinthios secunda (V, 13, 14) quodam loco sic loquitur: Sive, inquit, mente excessimus, Deo; sive temperantes sumus, vobis: caritas enim compellit nos: judicantes hoc, quoniam unus pro omnibus mortuus est Et paulo post: Omnia, inquit, ex Deo, qui reconciliavit nos sibi per Christum: et dedit nobis mysterium reconciliationis, quia Deus erat in Christo mundum reconcilians sibi (Ibid., 18, 19). IX. Quaero quemadmodum: non aliter quam nascendo, patiendo, moriendo, resurgendo atque in coelum ascendendo? Quaero etiam quod sit mysterium reconciliationis nostrae? Num aliud quam sacrificium quod per suum sanguinem summus sacerdos obtulit Christus? Videamus ergo utrumnam solus homo perfecerit: quoniam, sicut illi putant, Deus ab eo in passione discessit. Sed huic opinioni Paulus apostolus evidentissime contradicit: Deus, inquit, erat in Christo. Erat in Christo, non discesserat a Christo. Deus erat in Christo, mundum reconcilians sibi. Quemadmodum reconcilians? non reputans illis delicta eorum. An forte hoc stultis placet, ut per hominem tantum fiat remissio peccatorum? Quod cum etiam Judaei respuerent dicendo: Blasphemat: quis potest dimittere peccata, nisi solus Deus (Marc. II, 7)? ipse Dominus, Dei hominisque Filius, volens manifestare incredulis non esse solum hominem quem videbant, sed Deum etiam in quem credere contemnebant, et potestatem divinam homini quoque propter unitatem personae ejus ac praesentiae contributam evidenter ostendere: Ut sciatis, ait, quoniam potestatem habet filius hominis super terram dimittere peccata, tunc dixit paralytico: Surge, tolle lectum tuum, et vade in domum tuam (Matth. IX, 6). Ita Deus et homo, unus et verus animarum corporumque salvator, et exteriorem hominem morbo carnali, et interiorem peccati onere levavit. Deus ergo erat in Christo mundum reconcilians sibi: nusquam et nunquam deserens hominem, quem propria dignatione, nulla prorsus necessitate, suscepit. X. Ad Hebraeos quoque idem apostolus in ipsius Epistolae prima fronte testatur: Postremo, inquit, in his diebus locutus est nobis in Filio, quem constituit haeredem universorum, per quem fecit et saecula. Qui cum sit splendor gloriae, et figura substantiae ejus, gerens quoque omnia verbo virtutis suae, purgatione peccatorum a se facta, sedit in dextera majestatis in excelsis (Hebr. I, 2, 3). Ipse ergo Filius Dei et filius hominis, unus est atque idem, qui propter aeternitatem cum Patre fecit saecula, propter incommutabilem lucem splendor est gloriae, propter aequalitatem figura est substantiae, propter majestatem gerit omnia verbo virtutis. Ipse etiam propter suscepti hominis passionem, peccatorum nostrorum fecit purgationem; et propte remunerationem, habet in Patris dextera sessionem. Quomodo autem purgationem fecit peccatorum, nisi delens chirographum, quod adversum nos fuerat (Col. II, 14), diabolo accusante conscriptum? quomodo delevit, nisi cruci affigens, et sanguine innocente diluens? Quod ergo olim Deus locutus est patribus in prophetis, et postremo est testificatus in Filio (Hebr. I, 1, 2), hoc credamus, hoc teneamus, hoc omnibus viribus defendamus. Accedit ad causam, quod tunc principatus et potestates exspoliavit fiducialiter, triumphans eos in semetipso (Col. II, 15). Quod opus non est omnino solius hominis, sed divinae in homine majestatis. Neque enim homo fortis et potens, sed Dominus potens in bello (Psal. XXIII, 6). XI. Item illic post multa, quibus Apostolus mysterium Novi Testamenti a Veteris figura discrevit, sic ait: Refragans legi Moysi, sine miseratione moritur in duobus aut tribus testibus: quanto magis videtur deteriore poena dignus, qui

Filium Dei conculcavit, et qui sanguinem Novi Testamenti immundum aestimavit, in quo sanctificatus est, et spiritui gratiae Dei contumeliam fecit? Novimus enim eum qui dixit: Mihi vindicta, ego retribuam, dicit Dominus (Hebr. X, 28-30). Quaero qualiter possit Deus Dei Filius conculcari. Videtis etiam hic quemadmodum nec dubitet, nec metuat, nec erubescat asserere Dei Filium conculcatum. Sed quoniam si quis sanguinem in quo sanctificatus est, immundum existimat, utique Filium Dei conculcat: ideo non discrevit hominis passionem a Dei majestate, cujus reum vult esse illum, qui pro nihilo existimaverit pro se sanguinem fusum. Non enim Filius Dei conculcatur, nisi in eo quod mortis quam in homine sustinuit, beneficium spernitur. Ipse quoque Salvator ac Dominus fidem remuneraturus interrogat. Videte quid dixerit: Quem me, inquit, dicunt esse filium hominis (Matth. XVI, 13)? Atque cum diversas aliorum opiniones illi suggererent: Vos autem, inquit, quem me dicitis esse (Ibid., 15)? me utique filium hominis. Ad haec Petrus, ab eodem inspiratus, et in hac confessione ad rectam fidem forma sui universis gentibus profuturus, adverte quanta et quam plena integritate responderit: Tu es Christus Filius Dei vivi (Matth. XVI, 16). Tu tu, o ille, qui te filium hominis dicis, tu es Christus Filius Dei vivi. Nunquid non etiam hic, sive interrogatione Domini seu in responsione apostoli, utriusque substantiae una monstratur ostenditurque persona; dum et ille se hominis filium, quod in aperto videbatur, edicit, et Petrus eum Christum Dei Filium, quod in occulto gerebatur, donata sibi confessione monstravit? Unde laudatus a Domino et beatus est dictus (Ibid., 17); quoniam non ei caro et sanguis revelaverit, sed Pater qui in coelis est. Quod ergo credere debeamus, Deus Pater per Deum Filium revelet, non caro et sanguis insinuet. XII. Post resurrectionem quoque, cum Dominum Maria minime cognovisset, et ille proprio nomine appellando, viam illi recognitionis aperiret, ac se tangere volentem ne faceret prohiberet; quid ei nuntiandum discipulis delegare dignatus fuerit, audiamus. Vade, inquit, ad fratres meos, et dic eis: Ascendo ad Patrem meum et patrem vestrum; ad Deum meum et ad Deum vestrum (Joan. XX, 17). Age nunc, eligat haereticus utrum putat, et cujus vocem malit hanc esse, ipse discernat: utraque parte acuto spiritali gladio ferietur. Ascendo, inquit, ad Patrem meum et ad patrem vestrum; ad Deum meum, et ad Deum vestrum. Si hominis vox est, ergo Filius Dei est homo ille: ad Patrem meum, dixit, ascendo. Si Dei vox est, ergo homo est Deus ille: ad Deum meum enim dixit, ascendo. Nec enim ait, Ascendo ad Patrem meum, et Deum hominis mei: aut, Ascendo ad Deum meum, et ad Patrem Dei mei. Qui igitur personam divinitatis humanitatisque discernit, utroque intellectu convincitur. Aut homo dixit, et idem ipse est Dei Filius: aut Deus dixit, et idem ipse est etiam homo susceptus. Qui enim dicit, Ascendo ad Patrem meum et ad Deum meum; repetendo meum et meum, unam probat polliceturque personam, quamvis distinguat utramque substantiam. Quod enim ait, Ascendo ad Patrem meum, pertinere quidem videtur ad unigenitum Filium: quod autem ait, ad Deum meum, pertinere videtur ad hominem factum. Sed in Christo Jesu nec homo creatus potest dici, nec unigenitus Deus negari homo poterit natus. Atque ideo nec Dei tantum, nec hominis tantum, vox ista esse convincitur: quam Deus et homo, unus atque unicus ipse filius, ad suos discipulos perferendam inseparabili omnino atque indivisibili mandavit affectu. Denique ut noveritis, et plenius advertatis ita esse quod dicitur, ad dissolvenda omnium haereticorum machinamenta et universas calumnias refellendas; ubi opus fuit naturam creatoris a creatura discernere, videte qualiter pro nobis pietas divina vigilavit. Vade, inquit, ad fratres meos, et dic eis: Ascendo ad Patrem meum et ad Patrem vestrum; ad Deum meum et ad Deum vestrum. Ecce hic evidenter ipsius Domini, id est Dei et hominis, a famulorum suorum persona distinguitur, et a natura vocatio separatur. Quamvis enim id quod mandatur, jam amicis mandetur et fratribus: ostenditur tamen quid Domino debeatur, quid servis caeteris tribuatur. Potuit namque dicere, Ascendo ad Patrem nostrum, et ad Deum nostrum; quia multum distat inter dominationem et conditionem, inter generationem et adoptionem, inter substantiam et gratiam. Ideoque hic non permixte nec passim dicitur, Ascendo ad Patrem nostrum et ad Deum nostrum: sed ad Patrem meum et patrem vestrum, ad Deum meum et ad Deum vestrum. Aliter enim illi Deus pater est, aliter nobis. Illum siquidem natura coaequat, misericordia humiliat: nos vero natura prosternit, misericordia erigit. Hoc enim egit ista divina humanitas et humana divinitas, tali ac tanto miraculo, ut hujusmodi gratiam indigna mortalium meruisset infirmitas. XIII. Et quis poterit, vel cui sufficiat paginarum sanctarum omnia uno in tempore documenta congerere, quibus sincera haec et mera veritas perdocetur? Sed et modus sermonis qui jam dudum excessit, aliquando tenendus est, nec mihi diutius laborandum cum eis, quos instruente Domino eruditos agnovi. Instate itaque, sicut Apostolus (II Tim. IV, 2) praecepit, opportune atque importune; et doctrina sana universos errantes arguite, revocate, instruite, roborate: non mea, quae nulla aut parva sunt, habentes in hac fidei regula documenta; sed Scripturarum divinarum, ac magnorum et doctissimorum virorum, qui haec ante nos et firmissime tenuerunt, et multiplicibus libris eloquentissime docuerunt.

The Scriptorium Project is the work of a small group of lay people of various apostolic churches who are interested in the preservation, transmission, and translation of the works of the early and medieval church. Our efforts are to make the works of the church fathers accessible to anyone who might have an interest in Christian antiquities and the theological, philosophical, and moral writings that have become the bedrock of Western Civilization.

To-date, our releases have pulled from the Greek, Syriac, Georgian, Latin, Celtic, Ethiopian, and Coptic traditions of Christianity, and have been pulled from sundry local traditions and languages.

Other Catalogue Titles for the Early Punic Church in North Africa:

Letters on the Council of Ephesus by Capreolus of Carthage (Aug. 2007)
Two Letters from Byzantine Africa by Liciinianus of Carthage (Oct. 2016)
Apology to Gunthamund, King of Vandals by Blossius Aemilius Dracontius (Feb. 2018)
Letter to Pope Theodore by Victor of Carthage (Feb. 2020)

www.ingramcontent.com/pod-product-compliance
Lightning Source LLC
LaVergne TN
LVHW051923060526
838201LV00060B/4147